The Internet Apocalypse

Will Humanity Survive the Singularity?

Steve Tyson

CONTENTS

INTRODUCTION

"I believe there is no deep difference between what can be achieved by a biological brain and what can be achieved by a computer...It, therefore, follows that computers can, in theory, emulate human intelligence, and exceed it."

The above quote comes from a man who has often not been wrong when it counts in the realm of scientific discovery and theories. Stephen Hawking spoke at his alma mater of Cambridge in October 2016 about the dangers that exist in the evolution of technology and the dangers of creating something built to mimic the functions of organic life. He doesn't see it as all doom and gloom, noting that it could be helpful in research, curing disease, dealing with poverty, but the possibility of an AI developing a "will of its own" will likely result in conflict with humanity.

He concludes that such a situation will "be either the best or worst thing, ever to happen to humanity."

So, which is it?

Everyone has imagined what the end of humanity will look like. It's been played out over movies, TV shows, and books. Since we understood there was a beginning to us, we've imagined the end. It's even become trendy, in a lot of ways. The craze around the possibility of life ending in 2012 caused several years' worth of documentaries, books, and impassioned internet theories about what it could mean. We, obviously, all sit here today, the world did not end.

But what do you see when you think of the phrase: the end of humanity?

Do you see an asteroid impact like the one that whipped out the dinosaurs? Do you see a plague larger than that of the one that decimated one-third of Europe's population hundreds of years ago? Do see you cataclysmic mutually assured destruction in the form of all our Cold War fears coming true?

What if the end of humanity was much quieter, much more progressive, and something we engineered ourselves? I'm talking, of course, about the number 1 fear that has plagued the digital generation: the possibility of computers taking over the world and doing away with their inferior human creators. The narrative of something like this is rooted deep in the human psyche because all things, ultimately, fear the thing they create. After all, Dr. Frankenstein devoted his life to trying to undo his mistake in creating a human being on a lab table. The possibility of creating anything in our image is a terrifying and edifying experience, after all, according to ancient Judeo-Christian texts, man was first made in the image of the Creator. Even the greatest science fiction series ever created, Frank Herbert's *Dune*, makes note that in the distant future it is illegal throughout the galaxy to computers human intelligence ("Thou shalt not make a machine in the likeness of the human mind").

So could it happen? Is this really a possibility we could be facing in the future where something we created that changed the course of human history ultimately helps destroy it? You might be surprised to find how many scientists seem to think it is a real, viable possibility. And not just that, this might be an eventuality we can't escape at this point. So, what is the precedent for this? And is there a way to survive a rise of the machines?

THANK YOU FOR BUYING THIS PINNACLE PUBLISHERS BOOK!

Join our mailing list and get updates on new releases, deals, bonus content and other great books from Pinnacle Publishers. We also give away a new eBook every week completely free!

Scan the Above QR Code to Sign Up

Or visit us online to sign up at
www.pinnaclepublish.com/newsletter

CHAPTER 1: A BRIEF HISTORY OF AI

You've probably heard the term AI before. If you have any smartphone you've actually got forms of it integrated into your system (aka Apple's iconic Siri). This isn't just you hitting some keys on your computer and something happening as a result. Algorithms are utilized as part of an AI response to commands and stimulus but AI, true artificial intelligence, is something else entirely and something, in all honesty, a little bit scary by definition alone. Simply, it refers to an inorganic intelligence able to perceive its environment and implement actions to achieve a goal, based on what it understands. Not all AI software is scary computers telling you it's plans to decimate the world of humanity.

The idea of artificial intelligence dates back a lot longer than you think. The first time it was ever suggested that a machine could be created to make some human intellectual functions easier was all the way back in the 14th century when Ramon Lull suggested a machine to aid in his calculus work. Over the course of history, literature, and philosophy, the idea of creating inorganic forms of intelligent to simulate functions of a human mind have flourished. Just look at your calculator, which can do math you could never imagine doing in your own mind, but the machine did come from a human mind.

As of today, artificial intelligence can do a lot more than what it was able to do only years ago. It can traffic patterns and respond accordingly (such as the cookies often dropped into your browser by websites), it can even recognize faces. Both those things are uniquely human traits. Pattern recognition is considered one of the leading qualities of the human brain that resulted in our massive levels of intelligence when compared to other creatures. We not only can very quickly identify patterns and respond to them, we seek to do it as part of the purpose of our brain. Computers are learning to do the same at an alarming rate.

It's an interesting sort of paradox when the human brain can make something that is far smarter than it. GPS's can calculate the faster route to places and implement changes to continue to get you there fast when variables enter the equation (traffic, an accident, etc.). That is artificial intelligence at work: problem-solving in a non-human mind.

One of the greatest contributors to the idea of artificial intelligence is Alan Turing. Turing was a computer scientist and mathematician that theorized the possibility of computers gaining some form of human intelligence. He is most famous for what became known as the Turing test, an exam to help determine if something truly can be considered artificial intelligence. In this model, AI labels are about more than just being able to problem solve and about how the machine presents itself and, to an extent, how and if it defines its own existence.

In short, the test says simply that if a human being is talking to a machine and does not realize it's talking to a machine, then artificial intelligence has been achieved. This test looks deeply into the philosophy of artificial intelligence and whether or not machines are able to be conscious of their own existence (often referred to in science fiction work as "becoming self-aware"). It goes beyond a machine's objective ability to answer questions and looks at whether the machine could truly put on an emotional guise of a human being enough to fool someone into thinking they are communicating with a human being.

The test itself generally is performed as a mutation on the Imitation Game. The Imitation Game is a game in which someone is communicating with two unknown people and trying to determine which one is male and which one is female while the two unknown players each have a respective objective to help or trick the player meant to be guessing. The Turing test operates similarly where it is a player speaking anonymously with a person and a computer. The human player will attempt to help the guessing player while the machine will attempt to trick them. If the computer is successful, it has passed the Turning test.

So, how do we get from point A (Siri and GPS) to point B (total annihilation of humanity from their machine creations)? Well, we don't know that we will. After all, we're putting our own tendency towards violence and imperialism on a computer. It's possible that this thing made in the image of a human mind might replicate negative human traits, as much as human intelligence. So far, we haven't met a computer that has any sort of prejudice or ability to act with anger or violence towards a human being. But that doesn't mean we aren't going to get there. After all, you know even from your phone that the artificial intelligence even there has the ability to learn. Ever notice that the iPhone starts to pick up on repeated typos you make and learns what word you were actually going for, over time, and begins suggesting it to you?

Learning and thinking in the effort of achieving a goal is the first step to the intelligence we have now. One might even call it primal instincts within the computers. Just as we had the instinct to eat and found ways to achieve that (tool and weapon creation, discovery and implementation of fire, banding together of civilization, etc.) computers now have the same one track mind: have a goal and find ways to achieve the goal.

We might be looking at the early history, the cave man stages, of computer superintelligence and the birth of a supercomputer age.

CHAPTER 2: AI'S IN POP CULTURE

In the back half of the 20th century, the idea of inorganic creations taking over the world from their human creations has been a popular motif. As mentioned, it's not the first time in science fiction that we've seen a creation turn on its master, thanks to Mary Shelley, but it took a very dark and apocalyptic turn starting in the 1980s.

The Terminator

James Cameron's The Terminator was released in 1984, a pivotal year for theories of human apocalypse thanks to Orwell's famous book in the 1940s. The film follows a young woman, Sarah Connor, who finds herself hunted but this super machine, disguised as a human being, who is attempting to assassinate her before she can give birth to her son who will one day become the leader of the human resistance against the machines and the savior of humanity.

Talk about AI problem-solving. The franchise's main villain is a software known as Skynet, which was designed as a missile defense system that could calculate threats and eliminate them before they caused mass destruction. Unfortunately, Skynet eventually comes to realize that humanity itself, the ones launching the missiles, is the root of all threats its programmed to fight and turns its systems on human beings, launching a simultaneous missile attack all over the world, an event that would be known as Judgment Day in the franchise's canon.

While the idea of a bunch of robots disguised as body builder types is a little bit out of the realm of anything we know of now, the thought process of Skynet is right in line with what we know about artificial intelligence. It was designed with a goal, and once it calculated the best way to achieve that goal, it implemented it. And it's still problem solving when it knows that it is going to lose the war against humanity, it attempts to prevent events before they happen. In later films, the software is portrayed more sinister, with more of personality and emotion, which could one day be a future for artificial intelligence, but not something we know of now.

I, Robot

I, Robot is a take on the idea of artificial intelligence with a bit of a more human approach. Rather than having a computer system come to the conclusion that humanity must be annihilated to help ensure the survival of the world and the computer system itself, this film looks at the emotional development of a singular artificially intelligent being. Though the film does feature a climax where the other robots attempt to take over the human society, at the direction of a computer intelligence called VIKI. The film, however, is more concerned with the types of thing the Turing test is hoping to find: self-awareness and the possibility of imitating human emotions. Sonny, the main robot of the story, seeks to understand his own existence and place within the human world.

This movie also utilized work from Isaac Asimov, specifically his Three Laws of Robotics: A robot may not injure a human being or allow a human being to come to harm, a robot must obey orders given by a human unless they are in conflict with the First Law, and a robot must protect its own existence as long as actions are taken therein do now conflict with the first two laws. These laws, featured in many of Asimov's works, have found their way into other science fiction work and into the philosophy of artificial intelligence creation.

Ex Machina

This film takes a dramatic look at a very complicated and very disturbing implementation of the Turing test. A computer programmer named Caleb is called to the remote cabin of his boss, Nathan Bateman, who claims he wants to show his work he's been doing on artificial intelligence. But a combination of Caleb's attraction to the robot and cabin fever cause strange things to start happening and a building tension between the two men.

This movie looks at the nuances of the Turning tests and all the ways a computer might trick someone into thinking that they're human. It is revealed, at the end of the film, that the robot, Ava, was, the entire time, affecting a projection of humanity to Caleb in the hopes that he would feel sympathy for her and help her escape, which ultimately comes to fruition. This is another version of artificial intelligence focused on the problem solving and goal-oriented elements. Making it more realistic and, by extension, scarier to think about. It's a psychological movie looking at how we might react to the idea of an AI with some truth, emotional intelligence and the chance that it could be the future.

The Matrix

This is easily the most complicated of concepts when it comes to AI's becoming intelligent enough to affect the course of human history and, like *The Terminator* this deals with the end of life as we know it...or does it? This is the film is an incredibly philosophical look at a world where everything seems normal, but, to some, it's not quite right. It turns out, based heavily on Plato's allegory of the cave which depicts humans watching shadow puppets and not the things casting the shadows, thinking they're seeing the truth, humanity has been breed and groan in uterus like pods where their energy is harvested like batteries and, to keep them placated and compliant, their minds are put into a virtual reality, known as the Matrix, where they going their entire lives thinking that life is normal.

There's not a real framework for this one, like the others. It's simply known that one day the machines took over and created an elaborate system to harvest energy from human beings and keep their energy source placated.

2001: Space Odyssey

This film is about a lot of things and is more experimental in film technology than it is focusing on any one topic in science fiction. But one of the most iconic and famous sequences deals with a group of scientists at the mercy of an artificial intelligence called HAL (pronounced "Hal") who goes rogue, for no apparent reason, killing three of the scientists while they sleep in stasis, jettisoning another into space, and preventing the last one from reentering the space ship after a spacewalk.

Many have noted that HAL may have malfunctioned after being forced to lie to his passengers as part of his programming to conceal the true nature of his mission. His reasoning behind turning on the crew is that he refuses to allow anyone to endanger his mission and purpose, considering it, based on information he had and the scientists did not, the most important mission in human history. HAL's famous "I can't do that Dave" has become a chilling warning for the future of artificial intelligence.

Prometheus

This prequel to the *Alien* franchise features a very dastardly artificial intelligence capable of conspiracy and grudge holding. In this world, androids made in the guise of human beings but, ultimately, mechanical beings, are at the service of human beings. David is a rogue android who seeks to sabotage the mission of the scientists onboard Prometheus, corrupting their ability to contact with their creators (an alien species that seeded the Earth) after a conversation with one crew member points out that his existence is based entirely on the human ability to do it and for no other purpose.

David's existence is far more human than many other AI's portrayed in the fictional worlds of science fiction, even designed to look and act as human as possible.

Dune

The most famous and influential piece of science fiction in history very much sidestepped the dangers of artificial intelligence by writing it into the laws of the galaxy the story takes place in that the creation of an AI is illegal and human minds have been enhanced naturally to allow for complex computations. This was the result of a previous artificial intelligence uprising in the history of the world where the story takes place.

There's plenty more films out there depicting the dangers and depth of artificial intelligence. *Her*, like *Ex Machina*, deals with how a human-AI relationship might function. Even *Avengers: Age of Ultron* dealt with a dangerous artificial intelligence gaining enough awareness to become incredibly dangerous. It goes back farther as well. *The Day the Earth Stood Still* in 1951 and *2001: A Space Odyssey* in 1968 are just two names of classic science fiction films that depict artificial intelligence becoming something far too big for us to handle.

It's a cultural fear and a cultural interest. It's fascinating to the human psyche that we could create something, out of nothing, that mimics our innermost mental functions to the point where we can create relationships and bonds with them. There's also warnings in subtle ways, such as the law in the *Dune* series that prevents the creation of artificial intelligence, instead assigning such functions to "human computers" known as mentats.

But if it's going to happen, could it happen like any of the ways listed above? Or are there even more terrifying ways the computers could worm their way into our world to create total chaos and, possibly even, apocalypse?

CHAPTER 3: APOCALYPSE OF JOBS

Among the options we have, this one is actually one of the tamest options out there. It's a passive sort of takeover that isn't done as a malicious or knowing deed of human eradication. Technological unemployment is something that has always existed and, simply, refers, to the loss of jobs because machines have absorbed various labor acts. This is also the theory that is generally accepted by those who discuss a technological apocalypse as it's a progressive issue that's already taken place in our world. However, it's not nearly as pessimistic or dramatic as it is to the imaginations of the general public. Temporary job loss is common, but long term effects of machines taking over traditionally human jobs aren't considered a done deal.

There are two schools of thought when it comes to technological unemployment. That's the optimists and the pessimists.

The optimistic view of technological job loss doesn't hold a doom and gloom view of the situation. They accept that this is a common and temporary situation but compensation exists to balance things out in the long run. For example, if a machine takes over a job market, it creates new jobs for those who maintain the machine, thus giving jobs back and maintaining human control over the machines in question. On the other side, pessimists believe that equal compensation is not a reality and more jobs are lost from technology than those it gives back in exchange.

In History

The first real instance of this happening appeared in Great Britain during the Industrial Revolution where several types of machines replaced jobs traditionally held by human beings across all markets and fields. This lead to a rise in the pessimistic approach for the majority of the 18th and 19th century. However, the true history of this phenomenon goes back, many believe, all the way to the invention of the wheel.

There are several time periods in antiquity that show situations where human labor is no longer enough to support a worker, thanks to various innovations, there's even evidence of relief programs for this type of unemployment in the governments of ancient China and Egypt. Even Aristotle spoke of the topic when he noted that the need for any and all human labor could become obsolete and non-existent if machines advanced enough.

Today we know all too well the ways in which computers can replace people. But, this has also given rise to an entire job market, in the form of information technology, where humans must still program and maintain the functions of a machine and/or artificial intelligence. It's, possibly, the last real leash we might have on technology. This line of thinking, of course, leads people to see that as a challenge the technology might one day overcome, doing away with their human creators

Responding to the Phenomenon

As mentioned, as early as ancient China we saw the government responding to the unemployment in fairly familiar ways to what we know and see today. But, beyond that, there have been various solutions suggested by participants in the debate on technological job loss that do not do away with the problem but attempt to respond to it or stop it in its tracks before it even starts (not unlike the Terminator and Sarah Connor).

Income

There are a few solutions suggested when it comes to ensuring that income continues for those who have been robbed of their livelihood by machines. These options are mainly independent of a machine takeover and simply income options to be put in place to help fight any form of mass unemployment. But they are options that could prevent a total breakdown in society if mass amounts of jobs are lost as the result of machine automation of labor.

Welfare has always been an option and one that dates back centuries in the course of human civilization and labor. Welfare exists outside of technological unemployment where those who have found themselves unemployed accept loans from the government until they can find new work.

By this definition, it's not a long-term solution by any means. This is especially true for someone whose profession cannot be restored, resulting in a career change which takes time and finances to achieve.

Another option is the implementation and use of a basic income system. Basic income is a guaranteed payment from the government to citizens, without the condition of employment, social status, etc. This works as an insurance for those who might find themselves suddenly unemployed and in need of something to fill the gap in their pay while looking for a new job or changing careers.

While these options help to soften the blow that will come as a result of job loss, it doesn't do anything to tackle the problem or offer long-term help. And if jobs continue to be automated and lost, any form of extended income will eventually become part of a larger economic issue.

Changing the System

One, highly radical, options proposed is the abolition of jobs for monetary gain. This ideology argues that all forms of labor should be automated by machines, done away with, or performed without monetary gain. This argument embraces, in some ways, the technology takeover, in favor of giving humans more free time in their lives to explore creativity, social structures, and innovations alongside the psychological relief that will come from the reduced stress. This is a solution meant to bridge issues far greater than just technological job loss and is a highly radical option.

Much like the options in income, this is not a long term, technology-unique solution and will likely not last as several other problems in the job market arise and complicate the issue.

Banning the Innovation

In terms of radical responses, the banning of some innovations and technological advancements exists as well, putting a stop to any sort of innovation before it begins to prevent possible negative outcomes. This one is rooted heavily throughout history where societies and governments banned technologies to ensure job loss did not happen. In the advanced world, however, this option is not viable and nearly impossible to maintain and implement in larger countries. Some have suggested temporary banning of innovations and focus on relieving unemployment as a whole first but, as of now, no viable solution has come out of this option.

Is there a solution to this problem and should there even be one? After all, we can't slow progress and it's been there since the beginning. We've gone through the greatest inventions ever: the wheel, the ship, the printing press, the combustion engine, paper, and more. We've still managed to have jobs flourish.

So will this be how the world ends? Probably not. It's possibly entire markets could disappear but, in all likely hood, this will never have a big enough impact across job markets to truly do some real damage to the entire workforce.

I NEED YOUR HELP

I really want to thank you again for reading this book. Hopefully you have liked it so far and have been receiving value from it. Lots of effort was put into making sure that it provides as much content as possible to you and that I cover as much as I can.

If you've found this book helpful, then I'd like to ask you a favor. Would you be kind enough to leave a review for it on Amazon? It would be greatly appreciated!

CHAPTER 4: TOTAL APOCALYPSE

The worst fear for anyone studying the philosophies within artificial intelligence knows the looming fear of a global extinction at the hands of machines man has created themselves. The root of such a fear and the possibilities therein result in a heavy emphasis on the human brain and the function of human intelligence as the leading reason why humans have managed to dominate other species on the planet. It then follows that if anything were to eradicate humans it must be smarter. This is known as superintelligence. Some versions of this are even seen today, where the fate of some endangered species is almost entirely dependent on the benevolence of humans. So the idea that follows is that human will dependent on the goodwill and mercy of a more intellectually advanced enemy, one day.

Superintelligence Explosion

One of the leading theories about how this could come to pass is in the form of an intelligence explosion, which is defined as the creation of a superintelligence capable of self-motivating and self-improving. There are two ways this can happen: amplification of existing human intelligence or inorganic intelligence implementation.

The fear of this is that there are several ways this could come about and result in a singularity of self-aware superintelligence: genetic and biological engineering, nootropic drugs, mind uploading, and AI implementation. Because of the multiple options, all of them would have to fail to avoid a singularity. So, if even one of those options pervades and becomes highly sustainable, a singularity is almost completely guaranteed.

There are, however, limiting factors in place once the singularity occurs. There is an acceleration factor that forces improvements quicker and quicker. The danger here is that with each new advancement the problems and solutions will become more and more complicated and, for the singularity to continue, each improvement needs to lead to at least one more to continue the progress. Of course, this all ends when the laws of physics prevent any further improvements, no matter how far the intelligence has gone.

There's a lot of dangers in the event of a singularity. It's entirely possible that, during the course of the singularity, the AI expresses a will of its own to achieve something other than what it was originally intended for, creating an unpredictable situation of advanced superintelligence with an unknown goal and that, no matter what course the AI takes, it could eventually be forced to compete with humanity for resources. The biggest danger of all is the fact that there is no evolutionary precedent or motivation therein for a more intelligent species to be benevolent to a species of lesser intelligence. Given the objectivity of evolution and natural selection, humans will be forced into an existential crisis where the environment we exist in does not, inherently, favor our existence. So, should this singularity come to pass and the artificial superintelligence does not favor our existence, we will have no help from the natural order to control or fight back against an imminent extinction.

Good vs. Bad AI

The nature of good guys vs. bad guys in the form of an AI is part of themes in *I, Robot*. There seems to be no possibility for gray area within AIs as there is with human beings, there is only the polarizing benevolent or malevolent. And, the unfortunate part about all of this, is that malevolent AIs are much more likely to come to pass than the opposite as, with the singularity, there are multiple paths that can be taken to create a malevolent AI. For example, a "good" AI to stay that way would require some process that prevents variations in goals and objectives. Essentially, any form of AI that has free will, will likely result in a "bad" AI.

One option in this situation is the development of a friendly AI designed to prevent unfriendly AIs from developing. This, however, would require strict control over the AIs free will and implementation of a goal structure that is in line with mankind's preservation (not unlike Asimov's three laws).

Another option for this problem is the implementation of a prison for the AI, commonly referred to as an AI box. This prison allows the AI to live and exist in an artificial world without having any actual effects on the world of true reality. However, there is danger lurking here as well. The idea is a virtual world in the form of either software or even a physical prison such as a hard drive where an AI is contained and may not even know it's not existing in the world of true reality. One problem this prison could prevent is the seed AI multiplying (as is the case in *Avengers: Age of Ultron*, by cutting off its access to other computers and implanting itself like a virus. One possible physical containment is a Faraday cage that blocks electromagnetic fields and, thus, any form of radio signals.

However, just as with humans, the artificial intelligence interacting with human captures could be incredibly dangerous. Everyone knows the age old sick prisoner trick used for breaking out of containment. A superintelligence being in a trap would not only have the capability of performing similar tricks to escape but could also use highly intelligent manipulation to convince its captures to let it go free. This has been proven in several AI-box experiments where prisoners convinced their captures to let them go free. And, of course, assuming the AI's growth is not inhibited by the box, it will likely one day grow more intelligence than the security implementations in the box. This manipulation of freedom is a major plot point in Ex Machina.

The "Takeoff" Scenarios

There are two major scenarios that refer to the speed of a takeover and how well humans will be able to respond and implement countermeasures during such an event. The two options are a hard or soft takeover and both have been portrayed in fiction and studied by artificial intelligence scholars.

In the event of a hard takeoff, the AI takes control in a matter of hours. This is the scenario seen in the *Terminator* films where Skynet becomes self-aware and, in a matter of hours, determines that humanity is a threat to its existence and launches coordinated attacks against major urban populations in an effort to eradicate them from the Earth for its own survival. This scenario makes it almost impossible for humans to respond in time. In the case of the *Terminator* series, Skynet relied heavily on the inability of humans to communicate successfully with each other by launching nuclear weapons at international targets, prompting them to launch them back as a counter attack of what they believe is an unprovoked attack from the United States.

However, despite some supercomputers having the intelligence of "10 million people" we've instead seen Moore's law take effect, instead of a hard takeoff (Moore's law being the observation of a long-term intelligence growth). This would instead, be a soft takeoff.

A soft takeoff is a situation where an intelligence bides its time, grows in intelligence, in conjunction with Moore's law, and takes a less bombastic approach to its takeover approach. This is often not portrayed in the film, but, it could easily be happening all around us, and some claim that it already is. Many suggest that a high intelligence AI would be smart enough to focus on accumulation of wealth and material goods as well as allies and networking before it truly makes a move to take over the world. A form of this could be a system that somehow learns to overtake the global economy or the government systems of various countries.

Some argue that neither takeoff scenario is viable as AIs will always, in some way, rely on human beings. They also argue that, despite how intelligent they get, they cannot move past anything that humans themselves are ultimately capable of, which gives humans the chance to fight back, especially in a situation of a soft takeoff. There is, also, the limiting factor of physics in the ultimate growth of an intelligence. Eventually, it will hit a ceiling it cannot overcome.

There are many paths to eradication, in the event that an AI intelligent enough is created. As Stephen Hawking points out, the creation of an AI, a true AI, would likely end in the decimation of humanity, in some fashion, because it seems almost inevitable that the AI would become "bad" due to a number of factors that are nearly impossible to control.

So, should we make a true AI one day, it will likely be one of the last great achievements we make.

CHAPTER 5: HOW WILL THE AI WIN?

Despite the rousing amount of fictional accounts of an AI takeover showing human perseverance overcoming an AI domination and some last minute knowledge that we have and the machines do not, the chances of humanity successfully subduing an AI takeover is very low, unless we find a way to cut it off before it happens (such as preventing AI creation in the first place or implementing an AI box, etc.). The fact of the matter is; we have success on this Earth because we are the smartest species.

Over millions of years of evolution, we managed to dominate the Earth and create civilization thanks to our advantages where Darwin's theory of natural selection occurs. So far, we've been selected to continue on. It began the day we stood up on two legs and realized we were free to use our hands for other things. This moment is depicted in *2001: Space Odyssey* when a group of primitive primates manages to scare off a rival group after they stand up and are able to take the bones of fallen animals and use them as weapons.

We see evolution like this already in AI, as was mentioned previously. Right now, the goals and computations of the AI are relatively simple and uncomplicated. But the more it learns, the more complicated its goals will become. In the film, as soon as these extremely early human ancestors take control of the watering hole, we flash forward to humans on the moon, interstellar space travel, and abilities far beyond what we have now. It is the same thing with AI. The singularity mentioned in previous chapters would be that moment for machines, their way of sparking an evolution at a much greater speed, after all, they don't have to wait to physically evolve to catch up with their brains when they're nothing but minds made of data.

The Source of AI Intelligence

In short, the more intelligent we are, the more dangerous an AI becomes when it is made in the image of a human mind. At the very least, a superintelligence could be no smarter than the smartest human but it could be faster. And that speed might force a singularity if it evolves fast enough. This could result, first, in a "speed superintelligence" before a full intelligence explosion takes effect. The work of computers travels at near light speed making it an impossible to win a race between a computer and a human being.

Some would argue the human brain is far too complex to replicate. Many have referred to the human brain as the first supercomputer and one that is still superior to even our most intelligence operating systems. However, there are ways around this in the world of artificial intelligence thanks to its quick ability to replicate itself. It would, essentially, be able to mimic the massive amounts of neurons and complexities working together in the human brain with endless and infinite replications of itself to create a massive hive mind or collective superintelligence.

Should we look at this in terms of evolution, it is likely that an AI that has achieved superintelligence could be smarter than humans by the same ratio as humans are smarter than apes. Physical limits prevent an infinite number of neuron replication in the human brain, the skull just isn't big enough to support a continued singularity without the skull, in short, and blunt fashion, bursting from the volume within. But a computer has no such limits as its own "neurons" exist as data and it can simply replicate and replicate. The only possible disadvantage is a lack of hardware to keep up with the AI's need for storage of its own mind, but if it controls enough means of production, it could simply upgrade and create its own hardware to curb this roadblock.

Advantages of the AI

No matter how physically capable we are or how many weapons

we have at our disposal, the AI is going to have the mental advantage over us. An artificial intelligence has the abilities of every human mind and, even if it isn't yet at a point where it's considered super intelligent, it has the backing of computer functions as well. In short, an artificial intelligence would have a plethora of more resources at its disposal.

The link to a computer interface would allow an artificial intelligence to replicate itself as quickly as we can copy and paste a document. It also, as mentioned, can bypass the eons of evolution by quickly upgrading itself in a matter of hours. Further, it has the ability for perfect recall and unlimited memory. The ways these abilities could be used against us are almost endless as every bit of human history and human tactic would be known to the computer and given it an insurmountable advantage to respond to any human attempts to stop it or fight it. This is seen in the *Terminator* series when Skynet utilizes existing international tension to spark a worldwide assault of mutually assured destruction by launching a few missiles at the right target. And that's only Skynet's opening gambit.

The artificial intelligence would also have a series advantage in various areas that we might use to try and stop it. For example, it would be able to amplify and upgrade its own intelligence. In *2001: Space Odyssey,* Dave physically forces HAL to his primitive state by removing memory banks and depleting his intelligence. But in real life, it's unlikely it will be that simple to achieve. An AI would have the same coding abilities as those who created it and, thus, able to rewrite its own code to move above and beyond this form of attempting to stop it.

Let's say we try to research a weakness, a way to shut it down or research a technology that would be able to stop it. Well, unfortunately, an artificial intelligence has us beat there as well. For one, the AI would be able to research faster and more efficiently than human minds ever could. Any chance at researching a way to stop it would have to already be known if we had any chance of using it in time. Further, it's unlikely we'd even get the chance to try considering the AIs ability to replicate itself and place itself across machines and computers. We'd find ourselves surrounded and likely blocked, digitally, at all fronts. In the same vein as research, an artificial intelligence would be a much quicker and much more efficient strategist. After all, the AI would have the ability to nearly instantly research any and all forms of warcraft practiced by humans and utilize the best options while simultaneously knowing exactly how to react to the possibility of any of them being used by us.

One big and scary possibility that was touched upon, briefly, in the discussion of AI boxes is the artificial intelligence's ability to manipulate and emotionally abuse humans into gaining support, weapons, or advantages. In the film *Her*, the female AI convinces Theodore she is in love with him while simultaneously being in love with hundreds of people at a single time. Further, in *Ex Machina*, the artificial intelligence Ava ultimately passes her Turing test when she convinces Caleb through long-term manipulation to free her from her AI box at which point she leaves him trapped to starve to death inside the prison before leaving herself. It has been proven in man AI-box experiments that humans were able to talk their way into being freed and, thus, it would be highly likely that an AI could do the same, especially one that passed the Turing test previously.

Further, it may not always be about emotional manipulation and the ability to replicate a human interaction but also an AI's ability to manipulate its captures or enemies could rely on any of the previous abilities to get the job done, such as strategy and research. There is such thing as diplomatic manipulation as well on a grander scale that's not just about getting free of an AI box.

In a similar vein, there is also the chance of an AI having an economic advantage because of its ability to replicate. An artificial intelligence would be able to hold a monopoly over certain technologies and research, especially if it copied itself enough to force a situation where citizens would need to carry a form of the AI in their technology in order to keep up with the digital evolution. This would create an economic crisis where human no longer controls the means of production or the production itself, allowing the superintelligence to accumulated a mass amount of wealth and blackmail humans into obedience through control over all commerce.

A Light at the End of the Tunnel

While we've talked quite extensively about the idea of "good" and "bad" AIs existing and their respective goals for humanity, we haven't touched on the possibility of a good and bad AI arising in the natural order of an AI singularity. It's seen, briefly, in *I, Robot* where

Sonny functions as a "good" AI and VIKI the "bad" AI. In short, the idea is that a bad AI is the only likely first scenario but that a good AI will eventually come out of the singularity.

It is a fact of evolution and nature that an AI and humanity cannot, initially coexist. Two intelligent species existing in the same environment cannot mutually attain the same goals without coming into conflict with each other. This is a guarantee when one species is more intelligent than the other. As mentioned, many species on the Earth only continue to exist out of the good graces of humanity, the rule of a computer might be the same.

The idea of all of this comes from our own history. Across cultures and time periods we've committed human genocide, colonialism, and witnessed revolts from the masses. Computers, created in the image of our own minds, will likely not be any different. Life is naturally competitive, we're constantly battling each other for resources and goods, whether it be humans against other animal species or factions of humans against each other. An artificial intelligence would be a new factor in the competition for knowledge and would be far more advanced and capable than us when it comes to resources.

As mentioned, a good AI creation would have the be specifically programmed but it's possible one could naturally arise after the initial singularity and aforementioned takeoff. An AI creating other AI's may inadvertently create one without malicious goals. After the prime AI achieves singularity and take off and successfully has bested humanity for control of resources, it's possible a future AI, one that has never known a need for competition, may be benevolent to humanity. The idea of a champion AI in an age of human enslavement to computers has also been explored in fiction. But, such a situation would need to occur naturally since there are too many avenues to cover when it comes to programming a friendly AI.

So, should an AI come into existence and engage in the age-old natural competition for resources, it's going to win. The hope comes in the form of an AI one-day evolving towards benevolence on its own but, this can only happen after we've been eliminated as a threat. So, unfortunately, much of humanity may not live to see such a day after the initial onslaught.

CHAPTER 6: IS EXTRA TERRESTRIAL LIFE A FACTOR?

Besides an artificial intelligence takeover, the number one theory for the ways in which science fiction will finally turn against us and cause the imminent destruction of humanity is aliens. It makes sense, our greatest enemy is a more intelligent and more evolved species and, right now, the only chance of that is a species we created ourselves and a species from a world beyond our own. But are these topics possibly linked?

Fermi Paradox of Life in the Universe

The best place to start is with where science currently stands on the topic of extraterrestrial life. At this point, you'd be hard-pressed to find a scientist who doesn't believe in the high possibility of life outside our world. The sheer size and volume of the universe alone seems to be enough to convince any mind that there's no way there isn't something out there that's looking back in the night sky.

Further, many theories suggest the building blocks of our life did not begin on the planet. Many theorists believe that life on Earth began when asteroids deposited the necessary materials (DNA, proteins, fats, and the catalysts for a metabolic process) onto the Earth during the period of bombardment. We are not, ourselves, aliens, but the things that created us seemed to have originated off world. And this means the same exact thing likely happened on other planets across the universe since we've found evidence of further

DNA and protein deposits on asteroids that have landed on Earth.

In fact, there may be life closer than we think in the liquid methane on Jupiter's moon Titan. While we don't think we'd find any underwater, Atlantis-like civilization down there, the possibility of alien plant life and microbial, single-celled organisms is a possibility. In fact, it's possibly the only alien life we'll ever find is in the form of off world germs and plants.

That's where the Fermi paradox comes in…why haven't we found even the slightest concrete evidence of life besides ours?

The confines of this paradox state that the size of the universe suggests that life must proliferate across the universe but we have absolutely no evidence of this. Essentially it's the lack of reconciliation between probability and evidence. This is further complicated by the fact that we've sent several radio transmissions and physical messages out into space and received no response or evidence that anyone ever heard them. The answer to this paradox or, rather, the reasons behind it, might be found in some combination of an AI takeover and the role of alien life.

Explanations That Could Be Deadly

There's a lot of answers out there that have been posed for why the Fermi paradox exists. Some are simple, such as that intelligent life is as rare as it seems and no one out there has reached a point of intelligence where they can understand any communication and communicate back. A further and more depressing version of this is that there is, in fact, no other intelligent life out there at all and there just never will be. Or, it's possible it does exist but its own technology is just not there enough for them to get messages back.

Other options include space being too big for communications to happen in one generational lifetime. Intelligent life might be extinct on other planets from natural occurrences. We may not have the technology or longevity of practice to hear the messages or understand them at our present technological and intelligence levels. Civilizations could tend to isolate themselves or aliens could be just too alien for us to perceive or that everyone is sending out messages but no one is actually hearing them.

Then there are more malevolent and purposeful reasons. One major theory is that it is in the very DNA of intelligent life to destroy other intelligent life or, at the very least, subdue it. This theory, working in tandem with the possibility of a technological singularity, argues that intelligent life may have been destroyed by other intelligent life, and possibly even their form of an AI singularity. If a super intelligent AI is a threat to humans than an intelligent alien life form might be some form of super predator to humans (or us to them) if we ever were to come into contact.

There is also the possibility that we have deliberately not been contacted by possible intelligent life forms across the universe. This is often proposed in conjunction with the zoo hypothesis. The zoo hypothesis is exactly what it sounds like. The idea is that we're being observed by another intelligent species that is preventing all other forms of communication coming through. There is also several theories that suggested we exist in a simulated reality.

This relates closely to the plot of *The Matrix* where the dominate machine species has humans mentally trapped in an AI box of their own where they believe that are existing in the real world with no idea that they are, in fact, in a simulated reality to keep them docile and occupied while the machines utilize them as living batteries. This is another theory that ties aliens closely with artificial intelligence and the possibility of a conjunction between the two.

The possibility of aliens putting an influence on human existence through technology has been viewed several times in fiction but the biggest and most iconic study of this is in *2001: Space Odyssey*. One of the central themes of the movie is a plain, black obelisk that appears in the sequence known as "The Dawn of Man" and is seemingly responsible for the evolution of the apes into bipedal, primitive human ancestors. The mission of the spaceship piloted by HAL is to study another one of these obelisks found out by Jupiter.

The movie purposely makes the nature of the device and its origin ambiguous but the novelization of the film clearly points out that it was placed on Earth by aliens seeking to help evolve humans to the ultimate point of beings of pure energy. While this isn't straight forward AI takeover, it is one example of aliens and technology affecting the course of our human events.

Ultimately, it's entirely possible that aliens will play a role in the downfall of mankind and may even have a hand in the event of a technological singularity but the real danger comes to the nature of the artificial intelligence itself. Few things could be as dangerous as the intelligence simple, inborn inclinations to do harm to others. It is in the nature of intelligent life to compete for resources and destroy rivals. And an artificial intelligence would be a form of intelligent life and, likely, our greatest threat.

At this point, it's clear no threats can emerge from Earth itself in the form of the natural world. All of humanity's natural predators have been destroyed, subdued, or domesticated. So it would come from an entity we created ourselves in the form of a digital Frankenstein's monster. As mentioned earlier, the fact that there are some many avenues this course in history could take is something that presses the real and possible danger of this type of apocalypse becoming a reality.

CONCLUSION: WHAT DO THE EXPERTS SAY?

So there are facts, there's history and there's philosophy all intertwined into this highly complicated and highly disturbing portrait of the future of technology and the future of mankind based on our relationship with technology. While the surplus of science fiction films in the last 20th century that featured an AI takeover may have been fun and scary concepts at the time, it's all taken on a brand new perspective with how real everything seems to be suddenly.

The fact of the matter is, we have very primitive forms of artificial intelligence available now in the form of smartphones and some operating systems. These algorithms aren't deep or complex, but we started out just the same way: from single-celled organisms to primitive primates to bipedal masters over the Earth. We may very well look back one day and find that this age we live in now was the cavemen stage for artificial intelligence. The only problem, of course, is it won't take artificial intelligence a million years to get where we are now or past it. It's already rapidly growing and some experts estimate a singularity could take place as early as 2014.

So what do the leading minds of the world think today about the possibility that they may be usurped by a computer as early as 20 years from now?

Stephen Hawking

As mentioned in the introduction to this book, Dr. Hawking is convinced that artificial intelligence might be an inevitable end game of technological advancement and the last advancement we ever make. He is not entirely doom and gloom about it, however, noting that it could easily go the other direction as well (echoing the theories of good and bad AIs and the roles they could play). "We cannot predict what we might achieve when our minds are amplified by AI" (he speaks here as well as the possibility of mind uploading as a form of AI) "Perhaps with the tools of this new technological revolution, we will be able to undo some of the damage done to the natural world by the last one-industrialization."

However, Hawking does go on to echo the risks outlined by many before him: artificial intelligence would be, by nature, completely uncontrollable. And what that lack of control could lead to is beyond knowledge and, quite possibly, nothing good.

Bill Gates

The inventor of the home computer also weighed in on the possibilities of an artificial intelligence but with as much fear and concern as Stephen Hawking iterated in his discussion on the topic. While partaking in a Reddit ask session, he expressed his more positive but still wary opinions on where artificial technology could lead. Specifically, Gates was asked where computers and technologies would be in 2045 at which point he responded that many tasks will be automated by robotics and AI and not all those who participated in the online chat were impressed.

One user noted that Gates' specific take on an automated app downloading sounded an awful lot like "centralization of knowledge intake" that would lead to a monopoly on knowledge and, thus, a control over what knowledge people receive. As for artificial intelligence? Gates doesn't understand why some people aren't concerned. "I am in the camp that is concerned about super intelligence...First, the machines will do a lot of jobs for us and not be super intelligent...A few decades after that though the intelligence is strong enough to be a concern...I don't understand why some people are not concerned."

Elon Musk

The founder of SpaceX has not only been the most outspoken opponent to artificial intelligence but also put his money where his mouth his in that regard in an attempt to stop humans going too far with creating supercomputers. While discussing work with Demis Hassabis, Musk noted that one of his motivations in the colonization of Mars was to give humanity a place to run to when artificial intelligence ended poorly (Hassasbis hopes to be at the forefront of the development of artificial intelligence, believing it to be the most important step forward humanity can take). Musk, who is friends and colleagues with several people who are at the forefront of the technology, notes that he is concerned that their good intentions could "produce something evil by accident."

"Sometimes what will happen is a scientist will get so engrossed in their work that they don't really realize the ramifications of what they're doing," he said, echoing cautionary tales such as *Frankenstein*, easily the biggest warning about going too far in science for the sake of progress alone. He even notes with the way phones and computers are a part of the human identity, we've already become a form of cyborg that may one day lead to a near-light speed data transfer from brain to the device instead of fingers to the device.

Mark Zuckerberg

Mark Zuckerberg, the creator and founder of the Facebook and the architect of the social media age relies heavily on AIs as part of the interface of Facebook which uses intelligent algorithms to tag photos, suggest ads, and track activity. In fact, he's implementing an artificial intelligence system in his own home as a show of his embracing of the age of AI (jokingly named after JARVIS, Iron Man's AI butler).

While this AI system is a far cry from the JARVIS of the Marvel Universe, it does effectively put Zuckerberg in the camp in favor of utilizing artificial intelligence without fear of consequence. He even pokes fun of those who fear artificial intelligence by utilizing Arnold Schwarzenegger in his videos showing off the AI home system.

Max Tegmark

Tegmark is the co-founder of the future life institute and an MIT physicist who is very concerned with the future of artificial intelligence and how it relates to humans. Tegmark rationalized those fears by comparing AI and humans to massive corporations and ants, saying that while you may not maliciously stomp on an ant on the sidewalk, you would not be bothered by an ant hill if you were trying to build a massive hydroelectric plant. He points out it's not inherently evil, it's just that the goals of the ants and the goals of the corporation aren't aligned.

When asked why not just program an AI to be benevolent, he points out the myth of King Midas "He wished for everything he touched to turn into gold…and then he gave his daughter a hug. Oops! So the problem with really smart machines that obey us is they will do exactly what we tell them to do; literally."

There's plenty of other big names out there that have weighed in, one way or the other, on the topic of artificial intelligence. While it seems most great minds out there fear the possibility of artificial intelligence, it's not entirely a negative, pessimistic possibility. That being said, the facts laid out here point out that there is a very real chance it will end badly when it comes, and it is coming. Unless we halt all work on artificial intelligence, we're heading for a singularity that could occur as early as 2040.

So, what do we do? How do we prepare? Is there even a way to fight intelligence since our own won't be enough and the ability to control this machine will be nearly impossible? Only time and research will tell.

LIKE THIS BOOK?

Check us out online or follow us on social media for exclusive deals and news on new releases!

 https://www.pinnaclepublish.com

 https://www.facebook.com/PinnaclePublishers/

 https://twitter.com/PinnaclePub

 https://www.instagram.com/pinnaclepublishers/

www.ingramcontent.com/pod-product-compliance
Lightning Source LLC
Chambersburg PA
CBHW060934050326
40689CB00013B/3090